From the Hood to Doing Good—real life lessons from the young life of author Johnny Wimbrey. He gathers up his past adversities and formulates a new beginning. It's the experiences, not the years, that have surrendered wisdom to this young author, and from his adversity comes a success formula that will work for you too. "We all deserve a second chance," he says. Well, here is your chance to jump ahead in short order. Grab this book, read it tonight, and put the lessons into practice tomorrow!

ANDREW CAUTHEN, CHIEF MARKETING OFFICER
U.S. HEALTH ADVISORS, VICE CHAIRMAN
AMERICAN MILLENNIUM CORPORATION

In every generation, there are special people born who have the ability to touch and inspire the hearts and minds of others. I believe that Johnny Wimbrey is one of those special individuals. Johnny has "fire" in his spirit, which inspires others to transform their lives and achieve higher results because he has an amazing love of, a concern for, and belief in others. Plus, he possesses one of the most developed minds I have ever met. When you read *From the Hood to Doing Good,* you will see the essence of Johnny's soul on paper.

AL JOHNSON, PRESIDENT
JOHNSON INFORMATION RESEARCH

FROM THE

HOOD

From Adversity to
PROSPERITY
Through the
Choices
You Make

TO DOING

GOOD

JOHNNY D. WIMBREY

BROWN BOOKS PUBLISHING GROUP
DALLAS, TEXAS

Dedication

To my beautiful wife, Crystal Wimbrey, my love and my best friend: I want to thank you from the bottom of my heart for all of your support.

Contents

by Les Brown

It has been rightly said: it doesn't matter where you start out; what really matters is where you are going. Johnny D. Wimbrey is a shining example of that reality. Using his life experiences, Johnny has proven if you have a willingness to do whatever is required and take the initiative to pursue your dreams, you can make some incredible things happen.

If you are willing to elevate your life beyond your circumstances, like Johnny has, and allow that to become your life mission, coupled with a strong belief in yourself and a power greater than yourself, the possibilities of reinventing your life and who you are now to who you can become are unlimited.

This book is designed to empower you with the secret process of success used by the rich and famous. Johnny takes you through a step-by-step proven method to transform your life and experience health, wealth, and happiness, which we all want. I found every chapter inspiring and enlightening, as I'm sure you will. Life for Johnny has, needless to say, not been easy. In this book he generously shares the road he traveled to escape mediocrity and poverty.

When Johnny addresses an audience he encourages them to not allow their circumstances to determine their reality. He knows what it's like to be clobbered by life, thrown to the ground, and have dirt kicked in his face. But because of his faith and a determined unstoppable hunger to make something of himself, Johnny broke out of the hood . . . and is doing . . . I might add . . . very good, and the best is yet to come.

Johnny, you've done us proud, keep on making good stuff happen. The mark of greatness is upon you. This book will change your life; I guarantee it. This is Les Brown; Ms. Mamie Brown's baby boy.

Acknowledgments

Each man is a hero and an oracle to somebody.
~ RALPH WALDO EMERSON,
LETTERS AND SOCIAL AIMS, 1876

Because this book is a reflection of where I came from and who I used to be to where I am now and who I am today, it is dedicated to a lot of people who played a role in my life. I must first thank my Lord and Savior because without HIM, I know without a shadow of a doubt that I would have been dead a long time ago. For Christ I live and for Christ I die! To my children, Psalms Noel Wimbrey and Hannah Joel Wimbrey: You are my why, and I pray for your success in everything that you touch. To my father, a REAL man, Lawrence Eugene Wimbrey, Sr.: I'm proud of you for all that you have overcome and accomplished. I have always loved you and I always will. To my mother, Phyllis K.

Baron (Super Mom): I love you so much; you are a survivor and a fighter, and I owe my survival instincts to you. To my stepfather, Tim Baron: You are the best thing that has ever happened to my mom, and I really thank you for ALL of your support and love. To my brothers: Larry, I love you, and nothing will ever separate us. Keep your head up. Willie, if there was a thirteenth disciple, it would definitely be you (there will be streets named after you); thanks for being a friend. And to my baby sister, Ronnietta: You are so special to me; please stay sweet forever. I love you!

A special thanks to Joyce Harris, for being a mother when my mother wasn't able to be there, and to Corey Harris, for accepting us and being a brother. Big thanks to all of my in-laws, especially Momma-D for being one of my biggest fans. To Pastor C. W. Gillespie and Dian Gillespie: I would like to send my love for sticking in there when everyone else gave up on me and counted me a loss as a youth. Sorry for all the headaches. A special thanks to my entire family and loved ones, for all your consistent support.

To Jack and Regina Crane, "Papa and Momma Crane," whose love, patience, and support made all the difference in the world. Thanks for believing in me!

My publisher, Milli Brown, my editor, Kathryn Grant, and my lead designer, Alyson Alexander, have been most helpful and reassuring in the completion and success of this, my first published book. I had no idea what to do, but they held my hand every step of the way, and because of them this book is a dream come true.

To everyone who has been there since Day One: Thanks! You know who you are. To ALL my partners in success, thanks for not expecting me or allowing me to be average! Thanks for all your love, support, and motivation to succeed!

Introduction

Insanity: doing the same thing over and over again and expecting different results.

~ ALBERT EINSTEIN

I am extremely honored to say that thousands upon thousands of copies of this book have been shipped to individuals across the globe. When you read the title of this book, you may wonder, "What is the HOOD, and how can I relate?" Like many others across the globe, you will quickly discover that we ALL have experienced the HOOD. Whether you are a CEO of a Fortune 500 company, or a teacher, a student, an entrepreneur, or just beginning your journey into the real world, I have found that EVERYONE can relate to the HOOD—Hazardous Obstacles Of Destruction. We all experience life's adversities in some degree. The question is how you will choose to respond. Your response is your choice; it is your "responsibility," which means your Ability-To-Respond. If winning is a possibility, why do some people perpetually choose to lose? You move from adversity to prosperity through the choices you make.

If you do the exact same thing today that you did yesterday, then your tomorrow will be just like your today. You must do something different to get something different!

Growth is a part of human nature, and change is inevitable. We were designed to mature and created to evolve. It is a human characteristic to want to increase or grow. Only when introduced to the reality of life's obstacles do we become fearful to move forward and advance. Many times we find ourselves gearing up and mentally preparing for the journey of success, whether it be spiritually, mentally, physically, or financially. We ALL were designed to thrive and crave the thrill of INCREASE!

When children begin to take their first few attempts at walking, they don't understand the "I can't" or the "what if" options. Although they fall down over and over again, they're not discouraged, they're determined. They're not contemplating other options; they don't know that other options exist. They're focused and ready for the next attempt. Could it be because they don't comprehend failure yet, or is it because they see walking as an achievable possibility? At some point in our lives we lose the capability to ignore the impossible, and we subject ourselves to the fear of failure. We begin to contemplate that success might not be our right when we learn that failure is an option. The thought of failure often paralyzes individuals from ever attempting to take the first step toward succeeding.

When you were a child and someone asked you what you wanted to be when you grew up, you may have said something like an astronaut, a police officer, a doctor, a lawyer, or you may have said you were going to be a dancer, a singer, a rodeo clown, or professional athlete. Your dreams had no limits because you had not yet been exposed to the reality of limitations. I can't remember ever hearing a child say, "When I grow up I'm going to try to be a doctor." Children don't understand the word try. A child will look you square in the eyes and without wavering confidence tell you, "I'm going to be a movie star." Here's the secret! A child's formula for success is, "If they can do it; so can I!" Children know that they can be taught to do anything. Children don't understand the possibility of failure until someone introduces the fact that failure is an option. Let's renew that childlike confidence. *Never let a person define what's impossible for you to do!*

Fear in most cases is a learned emotion. Although we were born with the natural ability to evolve and increase, our growth can be stunted when we are exposed to the giant opponent of every human being, the word "but."

—Example: I want to start a diet, BUT . . .

When you use the word "but," it cancels whatever you said before you used the word.

—Example: I love you, BUT . . .

"I love you" was canceled when you said "but."

In this book, you will learn how to cancel your fears, enhance your life, and feed your desire to succeed! My personal story proves that if I can do it, anyone can.

For example, by all logic, I should've been dead a long time ago. I was not supposed to amount to anything; I was destined for failure. Success was not an option for someone with my past. People think someone like me does not deserve a second chance. There were only two places for people in my shoes: prison, or the graveyard . . .

BUT!

Chapter

Where you've been has nothing to do with
where you're going.

~ ANONYMOUS

Great athletes prepare for competition through very intense trainings. They experience pain, sweat, and sometimes even tears, but their drive for success and the end results feed the desire to press on. They understand that by lifting weights and exercising they may have pain, sometimes injuries, setbacks, and difficulties, but they also understand they are in the development and maturing process that will get their bodies and minds prepared for competition.

Likewise, I have experienced the weights of life and have been in mentally and emotionally rigorous workouts for years. But you know what? I am personally thankful for every hardship, every trial, and every burden. These personal experiences have molded me to become the well-accomplished, relentless, and victorious man that I am today. I wouldn't change any of the experiences in my life for the world. Just as a champion's workout is more intense than the average, so was mine. I am a champion, and it's because of my emotional and mental growth from my life's weights that I am here today. The best way out of difficulty is through it.

One of my earliest memories in life was living as a child in a battered women's shelter. You always hear that the first impression is the most important. It's true! Like it or not, we are ultimately labeled or prejudged by others' first impressions. It kind of seems unfair, doesn't it?

Well, think about it. Pause right now and take a second to remember someone you met for the first time who really impressed you. I mean, as soon as you saw this person, you immediately knew that he or she had life at its best. When they walked into a room, it lit up. I mean, they had it going on! Now, I want you to think about how you felt in the very moment you saw the person who really impressed you. Did you feel alive, motivated, energetic?

Now, go to the complete opposite and think of someone you met for the first time who really didn't impress you AT

ALL. I mean, this person to your mind was a pitiful sight. When they came into your presence, the whole atmosphere changed for the worse. You may not even have known this person, but somehow, immediately it was obvious that he or she had issues.

Now, think about this person who didn't impress you at all. What did that feel like? Did this person make you feel down, negative, or drained? Did he or she affect your mood, even if it was only temporarily?

The impression in meeting a person for the first time has so much power or impact that it affects the way you immediately characterize a person. It also has the ability to control your mind-set, your ability to think or feel good or bad about them. What about the impact of the first impression of LIFE?

Life Is Not Fair!

Life sucks! I think that would be a fair first impression of my life. When I was three years old, my mother ran for her life with my two older brothers and me. I mean, we literally ran out of our house in Fort Worth, Texas, with no shoes on and no destination.

The government shipped us to San Jose, California, and

put us up in a battered women's shelter without my father having any knowledge of our whereabouts. It did not take me long to figure out that something was wrong with my life.

"Why do we have to put powder and water together to make milk? I see everyone else pouring store-bought milk from a gallon jug."

"Why do we have to eat on the kitchen floor when everyone else eats at the kitchen table?"

"Why does our money come in a booklet, and all the bills are different colors? Everyone else has green money and they aren't limited as to what they can buy. All we can buy with our funny colored money is food."

I was in the first grade and we were just beginning to experience a sense of stability in our lives when my mother decided to pack us up and move back to Texas. I was introduced to my dad, who was a stranger to me at the time. My mother and father never got back together, but because of my mother's financial problems at the time, my brothers and I were forced to live with my father.

After several months of getting settled in and becoming

comfortable with our situation, my mother picked us up, for what was supposed to be a short weekend, and took us back to California without my father's knowledge.

I'd just finished the second grade when my mother told us that we would have to go back to Texas to live with our father, but this time she could not come with us. There are no words that can describe the fear and emotions that we went through. She told us not to worry because she would be coming after us shortly.

We did not see our mother again until two years after that. There were months that went by that I thought my mother was dead. When we got back to Texas I was forced to repeat the second grade, and start all over, while living with a man I hardly knew.

"Life is not fair!" That could have been my attitude. Maybe it's yours too. Can I ask you a question? Whoever told you that life was going to be fair?

This is the trap: we believe that life is dealt to us like a hand of cards, and whatever you get is what you get.

Well, I have some breaking news for you. In reality, ladies and gentlemen, you are in complete control of who you are, where you're going, and where you end up. Your destiny is whatever you say it is. It is wherever you see yourself going. If you don't see it or say it, there is no vision, and where there is no vision, people perish. You are and will be whatever you say you are. (More on this subject in chapter 2, Speak Life, Not Death!)

In other words, where you come from does not necessarily mean that's where you will end up. A mentor of mine named Dan Mikals once told me, "At some point in your life you must flip the switch." What he was referring to was that until you yourself take action and flip the switch, there will be no change.

It took me many years to realize this fact. For example, all my life people always told me I was very talented and that if I did not use my gifts it would be a waste. I was constantly in trouble as a youth, in school and many other places. My teachers always told me people would kill to have the talents I had. My problem was I thought they were flat-out lying. I thought that's what they had to say. As if they were paid to flatter us. This used to really piss me off! I was tired of everyone telling me how talented I was and how I was a waste. I mean, they didn't know what I had been through. Although I was in elementary and then junior high, at that time in my life I couldn't slow down enough to think about talents. I was just trying to survive the drugs, alcohol, deadly violence, and whatever else I had to go home to.

Could my teachers relate to a father jamming a gun in their faces, threatening to kill them, or wondering if their mother is alive because they haven't seen her in two years or heard from her in months? I did not want to talk about talents! I wanted to survive! How could anyone see such big talents in someone so small and yet hiding so much pain? How could they ever realize what talents I had?

The reason I got so angry is that they saw something in me I didn't even see in myself. It really hurts when you don't see "it" in yourself. My "it" was success—the talent to believe there was a chance that I, Johnny Wimbrey, could become great! I never thought about the future; all I thought about was what I had to go home to.

> **Destiny is not a matter of chance, it is a matter of choice; it is not a thing to be waited for, it is a thing to be achieved.**
>
> ~ WILLIAM J. BRYAN

What is your "it"?

Is "it" your past?

Is "it" your race?

Is "it" your sex?

Or is "it" YOU?

The Moment I Chose to Live

It was Sunday evening, January 31, 1993. I had just turned eighteen a couple days before, and I was watching Super Bowl XXVII's halftime show. The phone rang and I answered it. It was one of my friends, calling to let me know that one of our homies from the hood was shot and killed the night before, at a local bowling alley. Although I had had friends before who were murdered, when I got this message I went numb.

Not only was I good friends with the dead man, I also grew up with the person who killed him. These two individuals represented two different groups in our area. We all went to school together, and we had all been fighting each other since the seventh grade.

In my mind, the real war had just begun. I was very angry and had every intention of retaliating for my friend's murder, but the gang all agreed to wait until after his funeral.

God works in mysterious ways! Friday, February 5, was the night of the wake. We all brought our guns to the church, prepared for anything. Then the victim's mother found the strength somehow to make her way to the microphone and speak to us. We were unprepared for what she had to say.

She began to tell us the story of a recent conversation she had had with her son. She said that Chris, "Mookie," had come to her a few weeks before, and told her he was tired of running, that he was ready to live right. He then had given his mother his gun because he was serious this time.

None of us knew about this incident, but looking back, we realized there had been something different about Mookie lately. When I saw the tears in his mother's eyes, and all the pain she was going through, I was further amazed then to hear her express her forgiveness to the young man who had killed her son.

I had a mental epiphany! Who was I to seek revenge for a friend who had been murdered if his own mother had already found forgiveness?

That night I gave my gun to the preacher. I told him I didn't want to live like that anymore, and I asked for help. I remember praying that night for God to send someone into my life who would help me stay focused on doing what was right. I needed a reason not to go back to the streets.

The very next day, Saturday, February 6, at the age of eighteen, I met the young lady who would several years later become my wife. I remember thinking to myself that this girl is too innocent for me, and I was nowhere near her type. But we were both immediately attracted to each other and became really good friends in a very short period of time. She lived in a middle-class area and had a very loving family.

I remember wanting to impress her and at the same time protect her from my past, present, and potential future. So I began to act, talk, and dress differently around her. We never went to my side of town because I was afraid of the possibilities of her getting caught up in a dangerous situation.

As time went on I remember beginning to think in a way I have never thought before. I began to wonder about my future. Where was I headed, and what could I offer this young lady if our relationship got serious? I valued our relationship so much that I began to change my lifestyle. She gave me a reason and a purpose for wanting more out of life.

Up to that point, I had no idea what possibilities even existed. I was afraid. I had never thought about the future; I lived one day at a time. Then, I gradually began to think about the future—my future. What did it have in store for me? Immediately, I began to sweat; my heart raced; I was covered in fear. Thoughts of settling down and the possibilities of ever starting a family of my own terrified me. I did not want my future children's first impression of life to be that of a struggle like mine was. I had a change of attitude, and like Dan Mikals had said, "You must flip the switch," so . . . I flipped the switch!

I was determined to be successful. I didn't care about my past anymore. I had a new attitude, and I was not going to let anyone or anything stand in my way. And the first person I had to get out of my way was me!

Once I made up my mind that success was a "must" and failure was not an option, things began to change: By the time I was twenty, I was self-employed; I became a temporary licensed independent insurance agent. With hard work and determination, within six months I was one of the top agents in the nation with a national health insurance agency. At twenty-two I was having my first house built from the ground up. It was a two-story, four-bedroom home.

Within one month of closing on my new home, on July 27, 1998, I married my high school sweetheart. I then paid off ALL her debt and put her through her last year of college. I told her from day one she would always have the option to work or not work. Needless to say, she has never clocked in for anyone, and she has been the vice president of our home ever since.

My goal for 2000 was to make a six-figure salary by the end of the year. By the end of May, I had earned over $100,000. I was five-and-a-half months ahead of schedule. I was interviewed on national radio stations and a popular television network as a young success story. Since then, I have conducted seminars around the nation, inspiring thousands and empowering the masses for greatness.

I don't say any of this to impress you, but to impress upon you—if I can do it, anyone can! Who would have ever thought that a biracial, young punk ex-drug dealer who could roll a perfect joint by the time he was eight years old, whose earliest memory of life was marked by living in a battered women's shelter because his father was an abusive drunk, could ever gain the attention of tens of thousands of people from all walks of life and inspire them to greatness?

> **Adversity causes some men to break; others to break records.**
> ~ WILLIAM A WARD

Why would someone listen to me? I don't have a college degree or some prestigious background that would qualify me to speak before thousands. I asked myself this question hundreds of times until I was becoming my own worst enemy. Then, one day, I read a quote that to this day has changed my life forever: "Adversity causes some men to break, others to break records." I began to say it to myself, and I still do every day, adding another sentence. "Adversity causes some men to break; others to break records. And I am a record breaker." As soon as I started to say that to myself, I began to break records. Are you a record breaker? Do you want to be?

What I tell myself may seem a little arrogant, but if you believe that, you are your own greatest enemy. There is nothing wrong with confidence. "Those who don't understand the difference between arrogance and confidence will always be intimidated by confident people." The fact is, if you don't believe in your own greatness, no one else will. How else can you be great unless you believe that you are? And how else can you believe you are unless you're confident in what or who you say you are?

I once heard someone say, "The best way to predict your future is to create one." I'm living proof that this statement is true.

God doesn't make mistakes; we do. The question is not have you made mistakes? The question is will you get back up? Your past does not equal your future. In spite of your past, there are still possibilities. Where you've been has nothing to do with where you're going! The reason they call it the past is because it's behind you. And although your past has everything to do with who you are today, it's not necessary to consult your past to determine your future.

I will go back to where I came from, but only to pull others out.

"The best way to predict your future is to create one." What are you creating for your future? Take control! You are a record breaker!

Chapter

2

Speak Life, Not Death! TWO

Death and life are in the power of the tongue.

~ PROVERBS 18:21 (KJV)

T he biblical book of Proverbs (18:21 KJV) states that "Death and life are in the power of the tongue." That's a very true and powerful statement. The very words that come from your mouth will produce either life or death. WATCH what you say. Whatever you say will become your reality. If you say you're stupid, you're stupid; if you say you're smart, you're smart. Whatever you say you are, that's what you are. You literally become whatever you say and believe you are. Henry Ford said, "If you say you can; you can; if you say you can't, you can't. Either way, you're still right."

I teach in some of my seminars that there's always a positive way to say a negative thing. For example, instead of saying "I'm sick," tell people you're in the process of being healed. Never tell another person that you're broke! Say, "My finances are in transition." I literally cringe when I hear people say things like, "It's just my luck," or "with my luck . . .". To me that is saying that you don't believe there's any possibility for good things to happen to you. There's nothing wrong with expecting great things to happen to you.

I remember the first time I heard someone say, "Look in the mirror and tell yourself you are great." I thought to myself, this dude must be nuts! He wants me to look in the mirror and say positive things to myself? I was Mr. Cool, and to me, looking in the mirror and talking to myself didn't come across as too cool. I remember not too long after that, I was at home brushing my teeth in front of the mirror. I began to think about what the man had said. I thought, OK, I'm home alone, no one will ever know. So I began to think, what can I say to myself that would be positive and self-affirming? Me being Mr. Cool and playing around, I looked dead into the mirror and said, "Johnny, I love you."

Instantly, the most incredible thing happened to me. I began to cry like a baby. I mean, here I am, home alone, crying with no explanation. At first I tried to compose myself and play it cool. And then I thought, hey, I'm home alone; Johnny, let it go. I must have cried for about fifteen minutes, with no understanding of why I was crying. I was twenty-four at the time, and what really happened at that moment didn't hit me until a few months later. As a man, I wasn't used to hearing another man tell me, "I love you," because I had never heard it from my father. The biggest revelation was this: until that moment I never really understood what it meant to love yourself. I had thought it was selfish to love yourself, but in reality, how can you truly love someone else unless you learn to love yourself first? At that moment I realized that if no one else said great things about me, I must say them about myself.

From that day forward, not a day has gone by that I don't take a time out to affirm myself. These are things that I tell myself on a daily basis: I am a great husband; I am a wonderful father; I am highly blessed and highly favored; I am the head and not the tail; I am above and not beneath; I'm blessed when I come in and I'm blessed when I go out; I will speak life; I will empower masses for greatness; I am a world changer; I am a man of integrity; my words have power to move mountains; I am a record breaker; and anything I put my hands to will prosper.

There are some who will think that these practices are arrogant. But as I stated in chapter 1, people who don't understand the difference between confidence and arrogance will always be intimidated by confident people.

You must believe that you are a success before success can manifest itself in your life. It's literally impossible for you to believe it unless you say it first.

Let's clear up some misperceptions. People often mistake money for success. There are a lot of individuals who have plenty of money but who have never experienced or tapped into the true definition of success. Money will increase any and every habit that you have. That can be a good thing and that can be a bad thing. If you have a habit of donating money to charities, chances are when your money increases, your donations will increase too. If you have a drug habit and your money increases, chances are your drug intake will increase also. The love of money is said to be the root of all evil. Don't let the love of money detour you from your success. Use money as a tool for good, a tool for giving back, for others, for your family and friends. But don't let it be the end-all of your existence. How will you handle your success when it comes? You need to be prepared, and you need to write those preparations down so that they are in your face every day. Who knows when you may need to be reminded?

The Mission Statement

I believe that it is paramount to write your vision and make it plain because where there is no vision, people perish. In my home I have a mission statement that sets forth the vision for my home and the legacy that I will leave. It says that we will speak words of life by encouraging, motivating, and empowering the masses for greatness. We will strive to accumulate great wealth through hard work and determination, while strategically employing our money to work for itself, so our children's children will have a great inheritance that will make them destined for greatness.

I charge each and every person who is reading this book— whether young or old, male or female, black or white or Asian; it doesn't matter—to write a vision and make it plain. Speak it loudly and with conviction at least two times a day, and see if what you speak with conviction begins to come to pass.

Read this aloud: "I WILL DO TODAY WHAT OTHERS DON'T, SO I WILL HAVE TOMORROW WHAT OTHERS WON'T!" Again, "I WILL DO TODAY WHAT OTHERS DON'T, SO I WILL HAVE TOMORROW WHAT OTHERS WON'T!" Again, "I WILL DO TODAY WHAT OTHERS DON'T, SO I WILL HAVE TOMORROW WHAT OTHERS WON'T!"

Ladies and gentlemen, it is very simple. If you say you will, you will, and if you say you won't, you won't. Take control of every word that comes from your lips, and take every negative thought captive. Separate yourself from negative people, and attach yourself to successful, positive, energetic people who speak life into you.

Les Brown once stated that the only thing more important than saying, "I can," is saying "It's POSSIBLE!"

I have always been the type of person to think, "If someone else can do it, so can I." I know that if it's possible for someone else, it's possible for me. You are a possibility! Reach high, dig deep, press through, and say it's possible!

You Can Do ALL Things!

There's nothing to fear—you're as good as the best,
As strong as the mightiest, too.
You can win in every battle or test;
For there's no one just like you.
There's only one you in the world today;
So nobody else, you see,
Can do your work in as fine a way:
You're the only you there'll be!
So face the world, and all life is yours
To conquer and love and live:
And you'll find the happiness that endures
In just the measure you give;
There's nothing too good for you to possess,
Nor heights where you cannot go:
Your power is more than belief or guess—
It is something you have to know.

There is nothing to fear—you can and you will.
For you are the invincible you.
Set your foot on the highest hill—
There's nothing you cannot do.
~AUTHOR UNKNOWN

Winning With Words!

Reneé Hornbuckle, founder of The Women of Influence Conference, made a powerful statement in one of her seminars that originated from Dr. James Dobson. She said, "It takes seven positive comments to cancel one negative comment." To me, that was a very powerful and chilling revelation. Think about it for a second. Can it be true? Could it really be that simple? Does this mean that anyone could literally take control of his or her destiny by canceling every negative statement or comment with seven positive ones? Could this assertion be challenged for validity? Sure, it could. I will be the first to tell you that I found it hard to believe. I'll also be the first to tell you that while researching whether this was a myth, I became a firm believer in Dr. Dobson's theory.

You have to understand that I am a realist. So it was very important to me to find out whether this statement, this declaration, if you will, had some truth to it. I began to look for someone to tell me something negative. I purposed in my heart that for every negative report I received, I would cancel it with seven positive ones. I was determined, I was ready for war, I was hungry, and I wanted someone to tell me what I couldn't do. Tell me I'm not the man for the job, tell me I'm not good enough!

"People who say it cannot be done should not interrupt those who are doing it."

~ Anonymous

You know, it's amazing, but I didn't have to look hard or long. There's always someone willing to kill your dreams and hold you back. I remember this as if it were yesterday. I was very excited because I had found the home that I wanted to build. I was only twenty-one, and I had never owned a home before. The one I wanted was a two-story, four-bedroom house with a two-car garage and two-and-a-half baths.

How many of you know that you can't share your dreams with everyone? I showed the plans to a couple who I really cared about, and I knew they were going to be happy for me. With excitement, with my chest puffed up with pride, I handed the plans to them and said, "Look at the home I'm going to build." As they began to look at the plans, they slowly peered up at me, and with a simple smirk they said, "This house is too big for you; it's not a reality. You don't have any credit, and it would be better if you started out with a starter home."

Ladies and gentlemen, that's all I needed to hear. The trumpets began to sound, and it was time for war!

I got in my car, and with fire in my eyes I began to say, "This is my house; nothing will stop me from getting this house. The land is mine, and I will build. I will not be denied!

I drove to the land I had chosen, and I began to march around it seven times as I declared, "This is where I will build my home! I will not be denied!" Every time I said this, I began to believe that nothing could stop me from getting that house. I was invincible and ready for adversities. I saw myself living on this land, and I began to speak of the land as if it were already mine. I literally forgot the negative comments I had heard, and I began to believe that there was no way possible I could ever be denied that house.

It wasn't until several months later, after being approved with the best interest rate possible and several thousands of dollars' worth of upgrades for free, that I remembered that someone had said I couldn't do it. I'm telling you, I forgot! I literally canceled the negative comment by replacing it with a repetition of positive reinforcements. It worked!

I want to point out something, because it's very important to me that you understand. The people who told me that I couldn't get the house were not saying it to hurt me, but only reflecting their own experiences. In their own mind they thought they were helping me. It would have been very easy for me to accept their reality because they were speaking from personal experience. Who was I to tell them that they were wrong? I had never bought a house before; they had. I had never had a house built before; they had. Reflecting back, it seems the reasonable thing to do at that time was to submit to their wisdom because, as I said before, THEY WERE SPEAKING FROM EXPERIENCE. However, I had already purposed in my heart and was prepared for any negative comment. I mentally equipped myself to counteract any such comment and cancel it with seven positive ones. I had no idea that the situation would be so extreme, but I'm glad it was.

Reneé Hornbuckle's message emphasized that whatever you say more about yourself becomes your reality. It is said that seven is the number of perfection. And what a beautiful thought and reality that if you simply say, "I can," seven times for every one time someone says you can't, you are unstoppable!

It's common nature for someone to expect his or her experiences to be your reality. I dare you to purpose in your heart that for the very next negative comment you receive, you will cancel it by saying seven positive ones. Someone will read this and say it is a myth, it's crazy, it won't work; or it is not real . . . But I'm here to tell you . . . It's Real! It's Real!   It's Real!   It's Real!   It's Real! It's Real!   It's Real!

Chapter

3

A friend is someone who knows enough about you to destroy you—but doesn't.

There are definitely many words and many ways to define a true friend. This particular chapter is not necessarily geared to give you a traditional definition of the words "friend" or "foe." You see, when I say friend or foe, I'm speaking of much more than just a person.

A friend is one who believes in you when you have ceased to believe in yourself.

~ ANONYMOUS

If I asked you what your definition of the word friend was, you'd probably say something like, "a person that I can share my deepest desires with," or "someone who's going to be there through thick and thin." If I asked you what your definition of foe was, you'd probably say, "an enemy or someone who's against you." You're right! Those are both fair and accurate definitions.

> ## A true friend is someone who is there for you when he'd rather be anywhere else.
> ~ LEN WEIN

But what I want to do now is to challenge you for a second. Let's be practical. Let's go back to the basics. Let's think beyond our traditional mind-set and think outside the box. If I asked a five-year-old child what a friend was, he or she would give me a simple answer, such as, "someone who helps people," or "someone that I like." If I asked that same five-year-old what an enemy was, they would probably say, "someone who's bad," or "someone who hurts people." Wow! Isn't it fun to reflect back on the basics? Our childhood innocence seems to be the misplaced treasure of revelation. Sometimes it's the minds of the young and innocent that hold the true answers to the obstacles and cancers of life.

Vince Lombardi, who in 2000 was named Coach of the Century by ESPN, would address his Super Bowl champions at the beginning of every football season by holding up a football and saying, "Gentlemen, this is a football." Even though he was talking to professional football players, Coach Lombardi understood that in order to stay brilliant you must be brilliant with the basics. I think to experience true victory over our greatest struggles and battles, we must get back to the basics.

A friend is something or someone who's helping you become everything God created you to be. A foe is someone or something that's trying to stop you from getting there. As I said before, a friend or foe is much more than just a person.

A friend is any person, any place, or any thing that's pushing you toward your destiny. A foe is any person, any place, or any thing that's holding you back from your destiny.

Yes, a friend could be a person, place, or thing that's building you into being a better person. Are the places you go the most building you into a better person? What do you listen to and is that building you into a better person? Who do you socialize with and are they building you into a better person? Could your enemies or foes very well be the things that you entertain most?

This is where it gets hot, and if you can't stand the heat, you might want to get out of the kitchen. I'm serious. This may be the point where you want to close the book. It's self-inventory time! We are going to go face-to-face with who you really are. Everyone will not be able to handle this, but for those of you who want to become a better person, you're at the right place at the right time.

Identifying Your Foes

1. WHO CAN YOU NOT CELEBRATE YOUR ACCOMPLISHMENTS WITH?

Identify your foes. You cannot fight your enemies if you don't know who the enemies really are. A friend once told me that I should surround myself with people who celebrate me, not who tolerate me.

For example, I remember how excited I was when I bought my brand-new BMW roadster convertible. I drove that bad boy right off the showroom floor. I was more than "the Bomb," I was the explosion after "the Bomb"! I remember wanting to share my excitement with other people and how challenging it was to even think of one person who would be genuinely excited for me. So I called my wife first. She was so proud of me, and that made me feel good because I knew that she was a true friend. She celebrated me! I also remember when I began to show some family members and friends my new car. But very few of them said they were proud of me.

I'm not saying that's what I was looking for, but even a dog needs a pat on the head every now and then. It didn't take a long time to figure out that there were two types of people in my life, and deep down inside I already knew which were which.

It's funny how we can sometimes subconsciously ignore the truth. It became obvious to me that deep inside I already knew with whom I could share my excitement and with whom I could not. With the ones I could, I noticed I was myself when talking about how excited I was. With those I could not, I noticed that I was always apologizing for my success.

Some of you might be asking, "What do you mean by apologizing, Johnny?" Well, what I mean is this: instead of me talking about the car and the luxury features that came with it, I began to talk about what a great deal I got, as if I bought the car not because I was successful and earned it but because I just happened to get a good deal.

If you find yourself explaining why you have something, or how you got something with great value, and thus compromising your success, then you are talking to a foe. Listen to me very carefully. I'm not saying that these particular foes are not your friends. I am saying they are not true friends, that for some reason, when you're with these particular people, they do not allow you to be who you really want to be. And in that reality they have the capacity to hold you back or slow you down from your getting to your destiny.

Identify the Enemy in You!

I once had the honor and pleasure of hearing the NFL's great Deion Sanders speak at an event. He said something that night that was so profound, it has literally changed my outlook on life forever. Mr. Sanders said that the enemy is "In-a-Me"!

> ### It is a man's own mind, not his enemy or foe, that lures him to evil ways.
> ~ BUDDHA

This was my personal moment for self-inventory. Did I really possess the capacity to be my own enemy? Could I be my own foe? Could I be the enemy, "In-a-Me"? After a serious evaluation of self-character analysis, I have come to the following mind-boggling conclusions.

It is my belief that building character is a never-ending process. During every moment of your life, down to this very second, your character is constantly evolving. You are now, and forever will be, in a constant character-building state. It is humanly impossible to stop the process of character building. What you see, smell, hear, taste, or touch in your everyday experiences is building your character. Although you may not be able to stop character building, you can control what's building your character. Everything you watch, everyone you entertain, and everywhere you go builds the content of your character, for better or for worse, and you can control that. You may be the life of the party everyone loves, and people may say you are a person of great character. That's what the people see, and that's wonderful, but the true definition of character is who you are when there is no one else around. When you're home alone and nobody is there to judge you, what do you find yourself doing? When you're driving down the street all alone, what are you thinking about? Whatever the answer is, that's who you really are. Are you satisfied with this answer? If you are, that's great; if not, what are you willing to do about it?

I remember that when I was a kid watching Saturday morning cartoons, during commercials this little cartoon character-looking thing used to come on and say, "You are what you eat." This commercial was promoting the consumption of healthful foods. In a nutshell, the commercial was simply stating that healthful food equals a healthy body. This is also true with character. Your character is developed according to what you consume or what consumes you. What do you watch on TV? What music are you listening to? Who are you listening to? Do you have healthy social habits? These are all questions that you should ask yourself (and answer) as you do your self-inventory.

The things that entertain you the most and the things that you hate the most, they are who you are. Is this beginning to make sense? Let me give you an example. For instance, I hate being around negative and complaining people. It literally makes my flesh crawl to hear people complain and let minute situations master them. You know why? Because of who I am. I'm a positive individual, and I love to be around positive people. I am an encourager, I love to encourage people, but negative, complaining folk love to share their misery. Negative people drain me, and I understand that about myself, but if I still choose to entertain negative people, this would make me the "In-a-Me." Why? Because I am responsible for understanding the difference between the things that are building me up and those that are tearing me down. And understanding this fact makes me hold myself accountable for the persons, places, and things I choose to entertain.

Once you identify the entities in your life that appear to be your foes, you had better make an uncompromising decision immediately to cut them off. I don't care who or what they are, once you identify them, let them go. The moment you begin to compromise this decision, that's the moment you become the enemy (In-a-Me) inside yourself.

You might be asking, "What if it's someone or something that I really care about, or a family member? Johnny, are you saying that I should have nothing to do with them?" No, but what I am saying is that there needs to be a season of separation. You can love them from a distance. (Please note: This does not apply to your spouse. If your spouse is your foe, then that's another book.)

You have to understand that this season is for you. This is your time for developing a passion toward creating a better you. In order for you to tap in to your destiny, you must go through a season in which you make it ALL about you. This is your time to really evaluate who is for you and who is against you.

I struggled big time with this! In high school I was Class Favorite, Most Likely to Be Remembered, and Homecoming King. My point is, I had a lot of friends who I felt really close to, but after high school I began to focus on other things instead of just hanging out. I didn't want people thinking that I thought I was too good or that I wasn't down with them anymore. I did not want to separate myself from my homies who I used to drink and get high with. I mean, these were my "Day-One Homies"! And what about my crazy family? "I know they're a little wild," I told myself, "and they are always talking about other folks and gossiping, but they don't mean any harm. I can still hang out, I just won't do what they do, and I won't talk about the things they talk about." Yeah, right! If you're thinking like I was thinking, then you are setting yourself up for a fight you will not win. It's that simple!

A Do or Die Situation!

I was twenty-one and convinced that I was going to walk the straight and narrow. At this point I was engaged to be married and doing very well financially. I felt it was time to take it to higher level spiritually, so I rededicated my life to God, and I threw away every negative CD and movie that I owned. I began to listen to things that were building me up and not tearing me down. I mean, I surrounded myself with information and situations that stretched me to become better. But I was not ready to give up my Day-One Homies. I believed that our relationships and the time that we spent together did not have to decrease in order for me to increase. Boy, was I wrong!

I remember it like it was yesterday. One Sunday evening during the summer of 1996 my homies and I were kicking it once again, but this time I was different. I wasn't drinking; I wasn't getting high; I was just there for the fellowship. A little time passed, and I thought, what the heck, one drink won't hurt. To make a long story short, by the end of that Sunday night I found myself running for my life on foot while being shot at with a street assault rifle.

I got into a confrontation with another guy. I even tried to walk away to my car to leave, but he obviously thought I was going to my car to get a gun. So he ran to his car, popped his trunk, grabbed this huge gun, and began to chase me down while frantically shooting at me. I dove behind my car and curled into a fetal position, determining that this was it for me. I prayed to God to give me another chance! He did!

It's not fun being shot at from only about ten yards away. I should have died that night, but by the grace of God, I did not. To this day, those bullets cannot be accounted for, and some who saw it say they don't understand how I didn't get hit. Association brings about assimilation.

Sigmund Freud said that you're a product of your environment. That night, I almost became a statistic of my environment. I made a foolish mistake: to trust and rely on myself instead of submitting to the reality that I must separate from some things and let them go. That night I almost died in the midst of being the enemy In-a-Me.

That night was probably the longest ride home I've ever experienced. I had a lot to think about, and I had a lot of decisions to make. I began to understand that in order to get something different, you have to do something different. I wanted something in life that I'd never had before, and I knew that in order for that to happen, I had to be willing to do something I'd never done before. I had to separate myself from any and all things with the potential to stagnate my growth toward achieving what I consider to be the definition of success. I had to cut some things off. It was my season for separation.

> **I count him braver who overcomes his desires than him who conquers his enemies; for the hardest victory is over self.**
>
> ~Aristotle

If you ever want to find out who your foes are, I dare you to call for a season of separation. They will expose themselves. When you explain your motives, your friends, on the other hand, will celebrate you. These are your true friends, and those are your foes. A person, a place, or a thing could very well be both your friend and your foe. I am very happy to say my Day-One Homies supported me then, and they still do today. Thanks, guys!

Never feel guilty for wanting to better yourself. You should never sacrifice your success at the cost of a foe. True friends will not be intimidated by your passion and desire to increase. True friends will support you in your season of self-inventory, which is your season of finding the real friend in you.

A Season for Everything

1. There is a time for everything, a season for every activity under heaven.

2. A time to be born and a time to die. A time to plant and a time to harvest.

3. A time to kill and a time to heal. A time to tear down and a time to rebuild.

4. A time to cry and a time to laugh. A time to grieve and a time to dance.

5. A time to scatter stones and a time to gather stones. A time to embrace and a time to turn away.

6. A time to search and a time to lose. A time to keep and a time to throw away.

7. A time to tear and a time to mend. A time to be quiet and a time to speak up.

8. A time to love and a time to hate. A time for war and a time for peace.

~Ecclesiastes 3:1–8 NIV,

Chapter
4

FOUR

> We may have all come on different ships, but
> we're in the same boat now.
>
> ~ MARTIN LUTHER KING, JR.

To Master or to Be Mastered, That Is the Question

None of us are immune to adversity, none are immune to temptation, and none are immune to life's trials and tribulations. Whether we'd like to admit it or not, we all fall short in life at one point or another. Every human being will experience the good, the bad, and the ugly. That's a reality of life. The questions are, what are you going to do about it, and when are you going to do something about it? In other words:

1. When you get knocked down, how long will you stay there before you decide to get back up?
2. When you receive bad news, how

long will you ponder it before you move on?

3. When you've been broken into pieces, how long will it take before you decide to put yourself back together again?

How Long Will You Decide to Be Mastered Before You Begin to Master?

They say confession is good for the soul, so let me come clean for a second. I, too, have a weakness. Yes, it's true! In the past, and sometimes even now, I struggle and have struggled with lost time. People who are not time-conscious frustrate me. I can't stand to be late, and I hate being unproductive. I value time because it's something that you can never get back.

I programmed myself to think that way a long time ago. You may be thinking that it's a good and successful habit—and I agree—but anything you don't master will master you. Although I programmed myself to be a time-conscious individual, I never thought to prepare myself for situations that could potentially be out of my control. This is where the problem lies. Good people can make drastically bad decisions when not prepared for an unpredictable change that's out of their control.

You have a very powerful mind that can make anything happen as long as you keep yourself centered.

~ DR. WAYNE W. DYER

Some situations may seem very small and trivial to a lot of people, but a lot of small, trivial situations can and do escalate to very regrettable and drastic situations. I remember my first conscious decision to become the master in my personal battle against lost time. It was a beautiful, sunny day in Dallas, Texas, and I was riding in my Z3 BMW roadster with the convertible top down. I was listening to some good music; I was at peace and in the very best of moods. Then, as it happens, I looked up and noticed I had missed my exit. Instantly, I literally began to feel my blood pressure rise. I went from peace to frustration in a matter of seconds. I told you this situation would sound trivial but you must understand that by the time I got back on course I would have lost at least a whole five or ten minutes. As you read this, you're probably cracking up but I promise you, I am not exaggerating. What's even funnier is that by this point, I had conducted seminars and self-help courses across the nation, and I had studied numerous different philosophies and personally participated in seminars on self-control. Yet, here I was frustrated out of control because I had missed my exit. As I exited and detoured through some back streets to get back on course,

I began to think about something I had recently heard that was still fresh in my mind.

"If you want to get over a negative situation, begin to find positive things in your negative situation." So I figured, "What the heck? I have nothing else to do; let's see if it works." In the midst of my turmoil and frustration I began to look for positive things. My first reaction was that there weren't any, but then I began to look for simple things.

I remember it like it was yesterday. As I drove up to a red light I looked up. As a car was passing me, coming from the other direction, I noticed that the driver was smiling. I said to myself, if I hadn't missed my exit I would never have been able to see that person smiling. Instantly, like magic, my frustration went away! Then I thought, "Man, this is cool." As the light turned green, I noticed that the color wasn't your normal green; it was like a fluorescent, brilliant green. And I thought to myself, that's the prettiest green light I have ever seen. If I hadn't missed my exit, I would never have been able to experience this beautiful green light.

Now I must admit that all of this was totally out of character for me, but it worked. I began to feel excited, almost as if I was in a competition to find positive things. It was fun! I became the master of my own pet peeve. They say a mind is a terrible thing to waste, and I say it's terrible when you don't stretch and exercise yours.

Taking Control and Moving On!

Every individual holds the key to the God-given ability to consciously decide whether to master a situation or to be mastered by it. Every individual also has the ability to decide how long he or she chooses to master, or be mastered by, a situation.

In the previous chapter we discussed the importance of understanding that there is a time and/or a season for everything. It is very important that you also understand that every season will and must come to an end.

As I conduct self development trainings and seminars throughout the nation, it amazes me to find that only 10 percent of most individuals' battles are caused by the situation, and 90 percent are caused by the inability to move on and simply let go. It has always been a personal struggle for me to watch a person wrestle with a situation that would immediately disappear if they would just simply let it go. It drives me crazy to see an individual be mastered by a stupid situation. There are a lot of great people from whom I purposely distance myself because they choose to be mastered by stupid situations.

For example, could a marriage come to an end because two loving individuals don't agree on how the toilet paper should be installed? How could a person be known as a loving wife and mother one moment and the next moment be booked for murder because of road rage?

Let's be real for a second! Toilet paper has never been the cause of any divorce, and road rage can never be the excuse for any murder. The simple fact is good people make stupid decisions when they choose to forfeit the right to master an obstacle or an adversity and become mastered by it instead. It is said that you can always measure the character of a man by the size of the obstacle it takes to overcome him. Good people become murderers every day—and good people are murdered every day—because of individuals who simply are not in control of their immediate emotions. Think about it: How many people do you think are dead or in prison either because of their middle finger or someone else's middle finger? I don't know the answer, but isn't it ridiculous to think that a middle finger could cause an individual's rage to escalate to the point of deadly force? How hard would it be for most people to prepare or train themselves never to allow someone else's physical gestures to control them?

What and/or who has the ability to cause you to lose control and step out of your character? When you hear the words "lose control," it's probably a natural instinct to think of individuals who are literally out of their minds or crazy. We hear phrases all the time, such as, "He really went off the deep end this time," "She just lost it," or "He just flipped." These are extreme examples, but we lose control every day.

No one can make you jealous, angry, vengeful, or greedy—unless you let him.

~ Napoleon Hill

Individuals who are not conscious of the fact that they are capable of losing control will adopt the habit of losing control. And one who adopts the habit of losing control creates a lifestyle of one who's out of control. On the other hand, control can be regained. For example, have you ever experienced saying, "I can't believe I just said that," or "I apologize for snapping like that"? These are examples of regaining control.

Are you conscious of, and willing to recognize, where you seem to be less in control? When and where do you master, and when and where are you being mastered? I believe if you practice mastering the basics—or what some would call the minor things in life—you are literally positioning yourself to avoid potential disaster.

I was once told that you should manage your weaknesses and master your strengths. I'm not saying that we will ever be successful at mastering all of our emotions and every situation, but I am saying that every successful step forward is a step toward being the master instead of being mastered.

Is it possible to be in control in a very intense and heated situation? Absolutely! Let me give you an example. Have you ever seen one of the NFL highlight specials? I mean, like one of those Super Bowl highlight specials without any editing, where you can actually hear what the football players are saying on and off the field. It amazes me to see a 300-pound man hit another 300-pound man on the field, see them slam each other to the ground and lie on top of each other, yelling and screaming insults at one another, while close enough to taste each other's spit. Then when the referee blows his whistle, it's all over; they simply get up and walk away as if it never even happened. How can someone who is so revved up with intense energy and competitive emotions appear to regain complete emotional, physical, and mental control?

The answer is simple. Obedience is better than sacrifice. The players are mentally conditioned by the coaches and staff to understand that the consequences and penalties that come from uncontrollable behavior are simply not worth the risk.
You know what's really crazy? The exact same football

player who has the ability and discipline to walk away from someone who's spitting in his face, screaming insults, while slamming him to the ground, gets arrested the next week for being in a bar fight with someone who simply says his team is sorry. Could this be the same person? Are the world's legal penalties not more severe than the NFL penalties? The real questions are who's coaching you and conditioning you to understand the adversities you will face in the real world, teaching you how to ignore and/or walk away from something that simply is not worth the risk? Is it important to have mentors to coach you in every area of your life? (We will discuss more about mentors in chapter 5.)

We are the only creation God made who holds the gift of self-will. This means that we all possess the mental capacity to obey or to disobey, to lie or to be honest, to love or to hate, and the mental power to will ourselves to personal victory. If we learn to be the masters of our minds, we will begin to minimize our experiences of being mastered.

> **Not to have control over the senses is like sailing in a rudderless ship, bound to break to pieces on coming in contact with the very first rock.**
>
> ~MOHANDAS KARAMCHAND GANDHI

Chapter

Winning isn't everything, but wanting to win is.

~ VINCE LOMBARDI

Success leaves clues. There are no coincidences to winning. No one wins by chance or luck. Winners win because they want to win. Winners think about winning all the time. Best-selling recording artist Nelly released an international hit entitled "What Does It Take to Be Number One?" The chorus line says number "two is not a winner and three nobody remembers." This album went straight to the top of the charts and made Nelly an international phenomenon. He wrote the song before he became number one in the public's eyes, yet he understood the concept of winning and attitude. Winners eat, sleep, and breathe the concept of victory—of being number one. If you want to be in first place, you first must see yourself there. You must sell yourself on the fact that you are a winner and that you are number one, long before it's obvious to others. "Faith is the substance of things hoped for and the evidence of things not seen." You must think like a winner in order to become one.

Terry L. Hornbuckle authored a book titled *See Your Future, Be Your Future.* In this book he talks about how important—and how necessary it is—for you to see your future in order for your hopes, aspirations, and goals to become a manifested reality. You must believe without a shadow of a doubt that you deserve to win. And you must practice seeing yourself as the winner in order to be a winner.

> **Only a man who knows what it is like to be defeated can reach down to the bottom of his soul and come up with an extra ounce of power it takes to win when the match is even.**
>
> ~ MUHAMMAD ALI

Voted *USA Today's* Athlete of the Century, heavyweight champion Muhammad Ali mastered the psychology of winning. Long before Ali was the greatest fighter of all time, he told the world he was the greatest. Long before the world knew who he was, he told the local gyms that he was the greatest. And long before he became confident enough to become outspoken, he told himself he was the greatest. Ali first convinced himself that he was the greatest before he could convince anyone else. What's more important to remember than any of the above is this: Not only is it necessary for you to continually remind yourself that you are a winner, it is mandatory for your opponent to see, hear, and feel your confidence in your own abilities to win. When your opponent begins to imagine you winning, half of the battle is already won.

> ## Other people's opinion of you does not have to become your reality.
> ~ LES BROWN

Who is your opponent? Like your foe, your opponent can be anything or anyone who tries to keep you from coming out of the box. My opponents are the odds that stand against me. Society and statistics tell us that because I'm biracial, was born in the projects, lived on welfare, had an alcoholic for a father, and came from a single-parent home that I supposedly will never have any control of what ultimately will determine my future. According to society, I was supposed to have suffered emotionally at the hands of my peers because of my undetermined race; I am supposed to be struggling with alcoholic tendencies; I'm supposed to be socially and economically depressed; and my ever experiencing a successful marriage is not likely to happen.

But my reality is very different. I could have had problems in school about my race, but it was obvious that I was confident and very satisfied with who I was. In high school I ended up being Homecoming King, Most Likely to Be Remembered, and Class Favorite. I don't have any dependency on alcohol, I live a very nice lifestyle, and my wife and I have been married happily for over five years and are still best friends today.

Listen very closely. Never let others' experiences become your reality! You are the only one who can officially determine who and what you will become. If you see yourself in society's box, that's where you will be. Never let anyone create your world for you, because they will always create it too small.

Am I a freak of nature? No! I am simply programmed by God to be the head and not the tail; to be above and not beneath anyone or anything. I was designed to win, and so I choose to walk with my footsteps toward my God-given right. I am mentally programmed to win. I am a record breaker! I am confident and not arrogant.

Everyone experiences hard times and struggles, but all winners have one thing in common, and that is that we don't like to lose. Society has programmed us to think that if you're having trouble in your marriage, get a divorce. Almost all situations have an easy way out, but the prize for the race is not always given to the quick; instead, it is given to the one who perseveres and finishes the race. Winners understand that through the thick and thin, we must win! Failure is not an option for winners. They say winners never quit. I can guarantee you a quitter will never be a winner!

A true winner also understands the importance of surrounding himself or herself with other winners. I have made it a personal goal in my life to constantly introduce myself to—and continuously surround myself with—people who stretch me. All winners understand that you must get out of your comfort zone. You can't learn how to swim in shallow waters. Don't be afraid of the deep. It's hard to move to a higher level if everyone around you is beneath you or on the same level as you. I don't mean beneath you as in you are better as a person than they are, because we know that we are ALL created equally. What I mean is, for example, if you want to become an executive at your job, then you need to expose yourself to the mentality of an executive. There are a lot of people who are, or have been, where you are trying to go. You cannot follow a parked car. Hang around winners and you will become a winner too!

The Importance of Having Mentors

Winners understand and value the importance of having mentors. I have found that in many cases people use the word "mentor" very loosely. A mentor, first of all, is someone that you know personally. You may admire someone on TV, but he or she is not your mentor unless you have access to him or her. You choose your mentor; your mentor does not choose you. You may be approached by someone who wants to put you under his or her wing and guide you, but until you choose to go, he or she is not your mentor. In addition, your mentor must accept the role, or he or she is not a mentor. A mentor should be able to correct you on the spot; you submit immediately and take heed of his or her direction. This is why you choose your mentor. Because the moment you begin to unwillingly receive advice, correction, or even open rebuke, then he or she is no longer your mentor.

Synonyms for the word mentor: Teacher, Adviser, Tutor, Counselor, Guru, Guide. Webster's dictionary defines the mentor as "A trusted counselor or guide."

In order to have a mentor, you must be a protégé!

Synonyms and definition of the word protégé: dependent,

student, disciple, one who accepts the charge.

You can have different mentors for different areas of your life. For example, you may have a physical mentor, a spiritual mentor, and a financial mentor. It's great if all of these are the same person, but it's not necessary.

How Do You Choose a Mentor?

1. He/she has something that you would also like to have or experience. Example: You play the saxophone and he/she is very good with the sax.

2. He/she agrees to mentor you.

3. He/she must be someone who can tell you NO!

4. He/she has a lifestyle you respect in every facet.

5. He/she must be someone that you can be honest with, no matter what!

In the multitude of counselors there is safety.

-KING SOLOMON

Mentors' jobs are to protect us. That's why it's very important that we be open and honest with them so they can tell, show, and give us everything we need that is in our best interests. True mentors will tell us what we need to hear, instead of what we want to hear.

Great mentors will inspect what they expect. In other words, they won't just tell us what to do; they will follow up or make sure we report our results. Mentors are not dictators but advisors who want us to succeed without sacrificing our integrity. Great mentors will never ask us to compromise good character to get to the top.

A great financial mentor will show you how to master your money, instead of your money mastering you. When your money tells you what to do, you are in trouble, but when you can tell your money what to do, you can and will experience true wealth.

I once read that open rebuke is better than hidden love. A great mentor understands that he or she must tell it to you like it is.

A great winner is also a great protégé who will apply the advice from the mentor that he or she chose. A mentor has every right to terminate a relationship with a rebellious protégé. Likewise, the protégé has every right to terminate a relationship with his or her mentor. Keep in mind, if you find yourself jumping from mentor to mentor because they are not what you expected them to be, chances are they are not the ones with the problems.

I will tell you from experience that there are plenty of times I have gotten my feelings hurt by my mentors, but remember, I chose them. Winners are not afraid of constructive criticism and understand that it takes iron to sharpen iron.

My wife Crystal and I are very blessed to have incredible marital mentors, Eben and Sara Conner, who hold us accountable to each other. We chose them; they did not choose us. They have counseled us on several occasions. I must admit that when I know I am right, I am very quick to call them to referee when Crystal and I are having intense fellowships (arguments). I do confess that the majority of the times I call them in so Crystal can get help (because I am right). Usually, I end up being the one getting the most help.

Did you know that it is possible to deceive yourself? Deception would not be deception if it were obvious! You can be off track and not know it. And without correct navigation you will eventually crash.

Crystal and I know that Eben and Sara want us to win in every facet of our lives. And since they have our best interests at heart, we agree to submit to their wisdom. Wisdom is the application of knowledge. So when they share their knowledge, as their protégés we must apply their instructions, regardless of who is at fault.

A winner knows when to swallow his or her pride in order to resolve a higher cause and/or purpose. Winners understand that it is impossible to win by themselves.

Winners MUST Win!

Winners don't see success as an option; we see it as something that we must have. Average people want to win, but winners must win. While the majority of the world is talking about what they want to happen, the mentality of the winner is focused on what must happen. As a winner, you must be able to convert every one of your wants to your musts. When you want something, it's optional. But when you must have something, it's non-negotiable. Everyone wants to be successful; only a very few must be successful.

So how do you turn your wants into your musts? I've done seminars across the nation on this topic. And when I ask the audience to give me a list of things that are a must in their lives, here are some of the common answers that I get.

THINGS PEOPLE MUST HAVE OR DO
- be at work on time
- pay bills on time
- eat
- bathe
- buy groceries
- pay taxes

Here is a common list of answers that I get when I ask for things they want.

THINGS PEOPLE WANT TO HAVE OR DO
- eat healthy
- exercise
- go on vacation
- pray every day
- give to charity
- spend more time with the family

OK, by now you should get the point. The only difference between the things that you must have or do and the things that you want to have or do is you. Your attitude determines your ability to succeed.

Typically, the things that most people see as a must are tied to negative consequences. For example, if you don't eat, you starve. Or if you don't show up for work on time, you will get fired. In other words, most people are programmed to perform in order to prevent immediate negative reactions. You have a why for all your musts.

On the other hand, there are the few who are driven by the thrill of success. These individuals understand that they must do today what others don't, to have tomorrow what others won't. These are the ones who have the ability to make things happen, and who are self-disciplined. It is very important to have a reason, or a why, for everything that you want.

EXAMPLE
I "must" be successful because I "want" to leave an inheritance for my children's children.

When you find your why in everything that you want and become passionate with a burning desire for the end result, your wants will become musts. Therefore, you must find your why for all of your wants.

Wants + Whys = Musts

↶ I MUST eat healthy to live longer.

↶ I MUST exercise for energy and for good health.

↶ I MUST go on vacation because I work hard.

↶ I MUST pray every day to stay spiritually strong.

↶ I MUST give to charity to save lives.

↶ I MUST spend more time with my family to show my love.

My cause is bigger than me, and because my wants have whys that are much more important than selfish desires, I am willing to fight for the end result. You must be willing to fight for the cause of your wants. It's hard to fight for something without a cause, so connect all of your wants to all of your whys so that all of your dreams will come to fruition.

Chapter

6

People of mediocre ability sometimes
achieve outstanding success because they don't
know when to quit. Most men succeed
because they are determined to.

~ GEORGE E. ALLEN

I once heard that one of the greatest regrets of people on their deathbeds was they wish they had taken more risks in life. Isn't that mind blowing? To think of all the things that one could regret, one of the greatest would be wishing that you have taken more risks. Not I wish I would have spent more time with my children or family or maybe even taken more elaborate vacations. I wish I had taken more risks. It took me a while before I got the revelation. How could not taking risks be so devastating? I thought about this and it finally came to me. To take the risk requires but a moment; not taking risks becomes a lifestyle. You have to do what others don't, to have tomorrow what others won't. Average people don't take risks, and average people live average lives.

He has not learned the lesson of life who does not every day surmount a fear.
~ Ralph Waldo Emerson

Winners are not afraid to take risks because they understand in order to win they must go further than the rest are willing to go. Risk takers are more afraid of being average than they are of being ridiculed by spectators. The only people who never fail are those who never try. You must do something different. You must be willing to go further than you've ever gone before. Dig deeper, push harder, and take more risks than you've ever taken before. And I promise you WILL go further than you've ever experienced before.

Wilma Rudolph was the twentieth of twenty-two children. Her premature birth started her off on shaky ground, even more than the poverty she was born into. The doctors doubted her survival. Then when she was four years old, she contracted double pneumonia, polio, and scarlet fever. Again doctors doubted she would ever walk without braces. Her paralyzed left leg hampered her gait, but not her spirit. At age nine, she removed the metal leg brace she had been dependent on and began to walk without it. By thirteen she had developed a rhythmic walk. Doctors said it was a miracle. That same year she decided to become a runner. At this point, no one doubted it, but they knew she would never win. She entered a race, and she came in last. For the next few years every race she entered, she came in last. Everyone told her to quit, but she kept on running. One day she actually won a race. And then another. She began to win more than she lost. Then she won every race she entered. Eventually this little girl, a frail preemie, who was told she would never walk again, who was told she would never win a race, went on to win three Olympic gold medals.

A winner is not one who never fails, but one who NEVER QUITS!

The ME Factor

In my training seminars I speak about the "You Factor." What is the difference between your colleague consistently making "Top Salesman of the Month" and you? Why does your brother excel in athletics and you sit on the bench? Why are you on the outside looking in? I call it the "You Factor." You have the abilities and just as much talent, but you haven't decided to work at it, or go for it, or train hard, or build your confidence, so YOU hold the reins. In this section, I want to twist those words and the ideas 360 degrees. We'll end up in the same place, but the phrasing will be different.

I have been very fortunate to meet tens of thousands of outstanding and incredible individuals from around the world through seminars and trainings that I've conducted. It amazes me to see and meet individuals who have overcome the most devastating adversities. Some smile and are full of energy. You would never know the obstacles and trials they've endured. Somehow these individuals were able to overcome life's hardships and understand how paramount it is to be victorious over any and all situations.

I was told this story of one woman (I'll call her Nancy) who was virtually abandoned by her mother at age nine. She became the mother to her six-year-old and three-year-old brothers. She had to avoid the landlord, steal food, protect, comfort, and entertain her brothers. Her alcoholic mother would show up at the apartment every so often with a different man in tow. After screaming at her daughter to clean up the mess, she'd disappear into a back room. Some of the male visitors gave them money. Some simply looked at them with a blank stare. Eventually, they went to live with their maternal great-grandmother. When she died, the children were sent to different orphans' homes.

But Nancy determined not to end up like her mother. She

hung out in libraries, reading as many books as she could. When she could attend school, she devoured the lessons and emulated her teachers. Nancy knew she was as good as anyone else. She just didn't have quite as many pretty things. She pretended she would become a gifted singer, who would be on TV, admired by everyone. She dreamed she would become a famous surgeon, saving the lives of poor children. She visualized she would become a great teacher, helping the disadvantaged (just like herself). And guess what! She became a great teacher and a gifted singer. Not on TV, but making a difference in the lives of the disadvantaged and poor.

The art of being wise is the art of knowing what to overlook.

~ WILLIAM JAMES, IN *THE PRINCIPLES OF PSYCHOLOGY*

Anyone who sees such victory is amazed and wonders how one could endure so much and yet be completely healed spiritually, physically, and emotionally. How can someone who has been through so much devastation and terrible experiences be on top of the world?

Then you have those who have experienced similar tragedies but are obviously stuck in the bondage of anger, denial, or depression. That young woman's brothers did not survive the hardships of their circumstances. One committed suicide; the other lives in an alcoholic stupor, a homeless bum.

So how do the ones who survive do it? The answer is simple, ladies and gentlemen. Attitude is a choice. The only difference, from those who triumphed over adversity and those who are wandering in the pits of depression is the individual's fight to resurrect.

I call this the "Me Factor."

Here's my personal example of the "Me Factor." I am the youngest of three boys. My oldest brother Lawrence (Larry) is two years older than I am; then there's Willie who is eleven months older than I am. We were all brought up under the exact same circumstances. We all had the same father, and we all had the same mother. We all ate the same food, and we all had the same economic status. The only difference between us was the "You Factor." Each of us chose different avenues to how we responded to our situation. My brother, Larry, is currently in prison for the third time serving a forty-year sentence for aggravated robbery. My brother, Willie, has been in the ministry since he was eighteen years old and will become the principal of a public junior high school at the age of thirty. I speak to tens of thousands of people each year, encouraging and empowering the masses to experience true mental, spiritual, and physical wealth. How did three brothers who were raised in the exact same environment turn out with totally different futures? The "Me Factor."

I love both my brothers with all my heart. We experienced many events from which most would not have made it out alive. Willie made his choices, early in life, by refusing to become a product of his environment. Somehow Willie decided to stand for what was right. He was able to say no to the many temptations we suffered and didn't make the mistakes that Larry and I did. Although we all had the exact same opportunities to make the exact same decisions, our choices to act on them were our own options. None of us are better than the other; we're all just different. Although I never robbed anyone at gunpoint, there are things that I participated in that deserve prison time; but I decided to change before I got caught. We three brothers are a lot alike. All three of us are very compassionate individuals, who would give the shirts off of our backs to help someone else, and our parents are the exact same way. There are things that we say and do that are just alike, but although we had the same opportunities to decide right from wrong, the choices that we made were our own individual ones. The way an individual responds to the cards dealt them is a personal choice, and that is what I call the "Me Factor."

I have trained sales organizations under the exact same

principles. When I was an upper-level manager in the insurance industry, we always started out our week with a Monday morning sales meeting, discussing the previous week's production. I found that my top producers always had a great attitude and happy stories of how they had such an incredible week. On the extreme opposite side, I found that the agents who didn't have such a great week always had excuses—problems that were anything but their fault. Agents who had poor productions complained about the leads, or the price, or how our products were inferior to the competition's. The fact of the matter is, every single agent in our division sold the exact same products; they all sold them at the exact same prices, while working from the exact same source of leads. The only difference between the top producers and the poor producers was the individual. Instead of wondering what they were doing wrong, they were focused on how the company and everything else was wrong. They should have been asking the top producers for wisdom and advice. They all were in the exact same office, under the exact same management, being trained by the exact same leaders. Why did they not all have the exact same result?

People who are on the bottom tend to point the finger at everyone else; it's never their fault. A wise person is one who applies taught knowledge and a fool is one who has the knowledge but refuses to apply it. Although many can be exposed to the exact same teachings and principles, the end result will ultimately be determined by the individual's choice of actions. This is the "Me Factor."

Instigators, Spectators, and Participators

They say there are three types of people in the world:
1. INSTIGATORS—those who talk about things happening.
2. SPECTATORS—those who watch things happen.
3. PARTICIPATORS—those who MAKE things happen.

Those who like to talk about things happening focus on problems. They are instigators and have no problem stirring up messes. They're always willing to throw gasoline onto any fire. Quick to talk about the problems, they hardly ever are compelled to search for solutions. They are the ones likely to be talking about how things could have been better. Individuals in this particular category don't possess the right answers, but they feel that they are qualified to point out the wrong answers.

Instigators are very unlikely to be on the inside of any major decision-making process. They are always the ones on the outside, wondering and complaining about what's going on inside. They have no desire to be in the game, but they always want to know what's going on. They love to participate in "tailgate parties." They are not interested in actually seeing what's going on, but they're always close enough to at least hear the noise. They will smile in your face to get a free ride. Instigators are people pleasers. They always try to please others at any cost.

Then you have your spectators. These are the ones who watch things happen. Individuals in this particular group will get as close as they can to the fire, but will never get in. They are just there to watch. Instigators and spectators have some similarities. They both are talkers with no desire to get in the game. Because an instigator is usually only on the outside, wondering what's going on inside, his or her information is usually passed on by a spectator.

Spectators actually see and witness the game firsthand; they have to see what's going on with their own eyes. Spectators can be very opinionated and sometimes even abusive. Spectators come to see two things. They want to see someone win, and they want to see someone lose. Although they claim to be loyal, spectators are known to turn on their own team in a split second. They are very emotional and quick to react. Even though in most cases they are not qualified to participate in the game, they are quick to criticize and judge the participants. Spectators need supervision and direction.

Finally you have your participators, the 5 percent who actually make things happen. These are the ones who are willing to get in the game. They are the ones in or on the field participating. Unlike the instigators and spectators, 90 percent of a participant's effort is dedicated to preparation for the game. They work hard practicing and perfecting their skills. They're constantly focused on winning. They are always prepared and willing to face any challenge.

Participants talk about solutions, not problems. They make things happen by addressing challenges with solutions. They are trained to ignore instigators and spectators. Regardless of what's going on around them and regardless of all the hype, they never get out of position. Participants are team players. They understand that breaking focus could bring harm to their fellow participants. There is no time for foolishness; they are focused on making things happen.

Each individual has the personal task of figuring out which category he or she falls in. You must make your decision today! Are you an instigator, always finding yourself talking about things that are happening? Are you a spectator, constantly watching things happen from a distance? Are you a participant in the game, focused on the end result (which is to win) and constantly bettering yourself by sharpening your skills and preparing to make things happen?

Summary

Anyone who looks hard enough for an excuse will find one. Do not let your past determine your future, because where you've been has nothing to do with where you're going. Speak life into your future and not death because whatever you say, you'll have. You must determine and be willing to accept that every individual has friends and foes. It is your personal responsibility to distinguish between the two and to disconnect from all that is holding you back. You possess the God-given mental ability to choose your destiny by every action that you display. Choose to be a winner today by seeing yourself at the top tomorrow. Think like a winner, believe that you are a winner, tell yourself that you are a winner, and you will win! Every day that you wake up is another day to "Make It Happen"!

> **I would rather lose in a cause that will some day win, than win in a cause that will some day lose!**
> ~Woodrow T. Wilson

It is never too late to walk into a new future. I used to think that it was too late for me to change my life because of all the baggage from my past. Then I learned why they call it the past . . . because it's behind you. It only takes one second to make a decision, and it only takes one step to start a journey of a thousand miles. Today is your first day; now take your first step. Make it happen! Welcome to your future!

If I can do it, anyone can.

Johnny Dewayne Wimbrey
MASTER MOTIVATION/SUCCESS TRAINER

Most Requested Topics

MOTIVATION/KEYNOTE:
Overcoming Adversity
Youth Enrichment
Leadership/Sales

MEMBER

NATIONAL
SPEAKERS
ASSOCIATION

A young, dynamic, motivational success coach, known nationally for his record-breaking achievements, Johnny Wimbrey has trained and encouraged hundreds of thousands of people as he participates in panels via radio, television, seminars, and events across the globe. Johnny's inspirational story of overcoming life's adversities has empowered the masses for greatness. He speaks on issues such as overcoming adversity, youth enrichment, mental breakthroughs, and entrepreneurship . . . to name just a few.

Johnny's young life was marked by one of his first memories of living in a shelter for battered women. Then he grew up as a young drug dealer on the hardcore streets. After several near-death experiences, he decided it was time to "flip the switch," and he refused to let his past determine his future.

At the age of twenty, and with no experience, he became a temporary licensed insurance agent. Within six months of joining the insurance industry, Johnny received recognition as a "Top 50 Producer" in a national marketing agency. In fewer than two years (moving from senior agent to district manager to regional manager, on to regional vice president overseeing Texas and Oklahoma), Johnny found himself training experienced regional managers to recruit, manage, and teach sales development skills for well-known national agencies. After recognizing the high demand for his services, Johnny decided to use his skills for a higher purpose. His passion is to create success stories by helping others experience financial, spiritual, and emotional wealth.

Johnny has been featured and shared the stage with world famous Les Brown, Zig Ziglar, Brian Tracy, Jim Rohn, Dr. John Gray, Dr. Denis Waitley, William E. Bailey, and Tavis Smiley, as well as many other great speakers, authors, and noted authorities from around the world.

Founder and president of "Wimbrey Training Systems," Johnny's message will challenge you to find your "Inner Winner Within." His message is simple: "Your past doesn't determine your future—and if I can do it, anyone can."

Contact

To request Johnny Wimbrey to speak at your next event and to learn about other products and services, please visit

www.JohnnyWimbrey.com